LEVEL 2

Animals That Change Color

Libby Romero

NATIONAL
GEOGRAPHIC

Washington, D.C.

For Miss Landes —L.R.

Designed by Nicole Lazarus, Design Superette

The author and publisher gratefully acknowledge the expert content review of this book by Michel Milinkovitch, University of Geneva, Switzerland, and the literacy review of this book by Mariam Jean Dreher, professor of reading education, University of Maryland, College Park.

The cover features a panther chameleon. On the title page, a white baby harp lies on the ice behind a dark-pelted adult. A veiled chameleon sits on the table of contents page.

Library of Congress Cataloging-in-Publication Data
Names: Romero, Libby, author.
Title: Animals that change color / Libby Romero.
Description: Washington, DC : National Geographic Kids, 2020. | Series: National geographic readers
Identifiers: LCCN 2019034684 (print) | LCCN 2019034685 (ebook) | ISBN 9781426337093 (paperback) | ISBN 9781426337109 (library binding) | ISBN 9781426337116 (ebook) | ISBN 9781426337123 (ebook other)
Subjects: LCSH: Camouflage (Biology)--Juvenile literature. | Protective coloration (Biology)--Juvenile literature.
Classification: LCC QL767 .R66 2020 (print) | LCC QL767 (ebook) | DDC 591.47/2--dc23
LC record available at https://lccn.loc .gov/2019034684
LC ebook record available at https://lccn.loc .gov/2019034685

Photo Credits
ASP=Alamy Stock Photo; DT=Dreamstime; GI=Getty Images; MP=Minden Pictures; NG=National Geographic Image Collection; NPL=Nature Picture Library; SS=Shutterstock
Cover: George Grall/NG; 1, Masahiro Iijima/MP; 3, Arnowssr/DT; 4-5, Freddy Lecock/DT; 6-7, Eric Isselée/SS; 8, FloridaStock/SS; 9, Robert Postma/Design Pics/GI; 10 (UP), Robbie George/NG; 10 (LO), Jim Cumming/SS; 11 (UP LE), Nick Pecker/SS; 11 (UP RT), Markus Varesvuo/NPL; 11 (CTR LE), Laura Romin & Larry Dalton/ASP; 11 (CTR RT), Greg Winston/NG; 11 (LO LE), Pierre Vernay/Polar Lys/Biosphoto; 11 (LO RT), Theo Bosboom/NPL; 12, Andrey Nekrasov/ASP; 13, Obraz/SS; 14, Geoffrey Robinson/SS; 14-15, Klein & Hubert/NPL; 15, Jan Woitas/DPA/ASP; 16 (UP), Terry Moore/Stocktrek Images/GI; 16 (CTR), Douglas Klug/GI; 16 (LO), Zen Rial/GI; 17 (UP LE), Jacky Parker Photography/GI; 17 (UP RT), Marcus Lelle/500px/GI; 17 (CTR), mgkuijpers/Adobe Stock; 17 (LO), Giordano Cipriani/GI; 18-19, Tim Laman/NG; 20, Stephen Dalton/MP; 21, DG303Pilot/GI; 22, Marcus Kam/SS; 23, Nilesh Mane/ephotocorp/ASP; 24, ifish/GI; 25 (UP), Trueog/iStockphoto; 25 (CTR), David Fleetham/ASP; 25 (LO), abcphotosystem/SS; 26, Stephaniellen/SS; 27 (LE), Dr. Jocelyn Hudon; 27 (RT), Premium UIG/GI; 28, Lexter Yap/SS; 29, Edward Rowland/ASP; 30 (1 UP LE), freeezzzz/GI; 30 (1 UP RT), Carl Johnson/Design Pics/GI; 30 (1 LO LE), Milan Zygmunt/SS; 30 (1 LO RT), archimede/SS; 30 (2), Michael S. Quinton/NG; 30 (3), Marc Anderson/ASP; 31 (4 UP LE), Gerald Robert Fischer/SS; 31 (4 UP RT), Norbert Rosing/NG; 31 (4 LO LE), Konrad Wothe/NPL; 31 (4 LO RT), Michio Hoshino/MP; 31 (5), Aroona Kavathekar/ASP; 31 (6), Lynn Whitt/SS; 31 (7), Mauricio Handler/NG; 32 (UP LE), Designua/SS; 32 (UP RT), Theo Bosboom/NPL; 32 (CTR LE), Jubal Harshaw/SS; 32 (CTR RT), michaklootwijk/Adobe Stock; 32 (LO LE), Gabriel Barathieu/MP; 32 (LO RT), Designua/SS; vocabulary box (THROUGHOUT), Ekaterina Nikolaenko/DT

National Geographic supports K–12 educators with ELA Common Core Resources.
Visit natgeoed.org/commoncore for more information.

Table of Contents

Living Colors

adult Atlantic puffin

Some animals can change color, almost like magic. It can happen in an instant. Or, it can take years. Sometimes the change is dramatic. Other times, it's gradual.

How do they do this? And why? If you want to know, keep reading!

young Atlantic puffin

Changing Moods

When chameleons' (kuh–MEEL–yunz) moods change, the colors of their skin change, too. How does this happen?

Chameleons have some skin cells that absorb certain colors. Other cells act like tiny mirrors to reflect certain colors.

When a chameleon is excited, its skin stretches. Some skin cells move. Others change how they reflect light.

Then the chameleon's colors change. When the animal relaxes, the cells change back to the way they were.

Cool Color Words

CELLS: The building blocks of living things like plants and animals

ABSORB: To take in

REFLECT: To bounce back

This panther chameleon is feeling calm. When it gets excited, its green skin patches turn bright yellow.

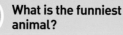

Changing Seasons

In the Arctic, some animals are brown in the summer. But they grow new white fur or feathers in the winter. Why? These animals change color with the seasons.

arctic fox

Can you find the arctic fox? It has a white winter coat of fur.

Days get shorter as summer turns to fall and then winter. This tells the animals' bodies it's time for a white coat.

Changing coats is a form of camouflage (KAM-uh-flahj). It helps them blend in with their environment.

snowshoe hare

Cool Color Word

CAMOUFLAGE: Colors or patterns that help something blend in with its environment

Can you find these animals in their summer and winter coats?

willow ptarmigan (TAR-mih-gun)

long-tailed weasel

Peary caribou

11

Growing Up

Scientists think a baby silvered leaf monkey's bright fur may help its mother keep track of it. It also lets other monkeys know that it is a baby.

Some animals change color as they get older. When silvered leaf monkeys are born, they have orange fur and light-colored skin. After a few days, their skin turns black. In three to five months, they grow dark fur with silver tips like the adults.

It takes about two years for baby swans' gray or brown feathers to turn white.

A Dalmatian's spots start to show when the puppy is about two weeks old.

Believe it or not, Dalmatian puppies are born all white! Dark spots form in their fur after a few weeks.

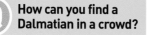

Q How can you find a Dalmatian in a crowd?

A Don't worry. They're easy to spot.

Baby harp seals are white, too. As they grow, their fur turns gray and then gets dark spots.

Tapirs do the opposite. As they grow older, their patterns disappear.

A baby tapir has white stripes and spots to help it blend in with the forest floor.

The baby harp seal's furry coat keeps it warm and provides camouflage in the snow.

6 Cool Color Changers

Cells in a peacock flounder's skin are somehow connected to its eyes. The brown fish changes to match the color it sees. If a flounder loses its sight, it can't change color.

1

Cuttlefish, octopuses, and squid all change color. They match their background within seconds—even though they are color-blind.

2

East Pacific red octopus

When a flamingo's feather falls out, the feather slowly loses its pink color.

3

4

Whitebanded crab spiders are white. But when females move to yellow flowers to hunt, they become yellow in just three days. If they move to a white flower, they turn white again.

5

Forget about blending in! Chameleons flash bright colors when they want to defend territory or attract mates.

6

Seahorses are so good at camouflage that scientists have a hard time telling one kind from another!

Hidden Colors

Some animals keep their colors hidden ... until the time is just right.

The male superb bird of paradise is mostly black. But he has shiny blue feathers on his breast and head. When a possible mate is near, he puts on a show! He flips his feathers to make a blue-and-black smiley face.

The male superb bird of paradise has blue feathers on his chest (right). When a mate is near, he rolls his black neck feathers forward like a cape behind the blue feathers (below).

19

The blue morpho butterfly's wings can be up to eight inches across. It is one of the biggest butterflies in the world!

The blue morpho butterfly has hidden colors, too. Its wings are brown on one side and bright blue on the other.

On the ground, when the butterfly closes its wings, it looks like a brown leaf. But when it flies, its wings flash blue and brown. That makes the butterfly seem to disappear in the sky.

Hide-and-Seek

The liquid inside the shell makes this beetle look golden.

Sometimes changing color helps animals hide right in front of predators.

The golden tortoise beetle has a see-through shell with grooves that hold liquid. The liquid helps give it a golden look. If a hungry animal comes near, the beetle drains the liquid. The predator sees the red body under the beetle's shell. Now the beetle looks like a poisonous ladybug. It fools the predator!

This golden tortoise beetle has drained the liquid from its shell.

Cuttlefish can change colors and patterns to match their environment.

Cuttlefish have millions of color cells in their skin. When a predator is near, the cuttlefish squeezes and relaxes muscles around the cells. This changes how the cuttlefish looks.

The mimic octopus changes color the same way. But it is also a master shape-shifter. It uses color, shape, and behavior to fool predators.

mimic octopus

mimic octopus copying a sea snake

The mimic octopus can copy the color and shape of a lot of things in its environment, like a stingray or a deadly sea snake!

sea snake

You Are What You Eat

Different species of flamingos can be shades of pink, red, and even orange. The healthier any flamingo in the wild is, the brighter its colors will be.

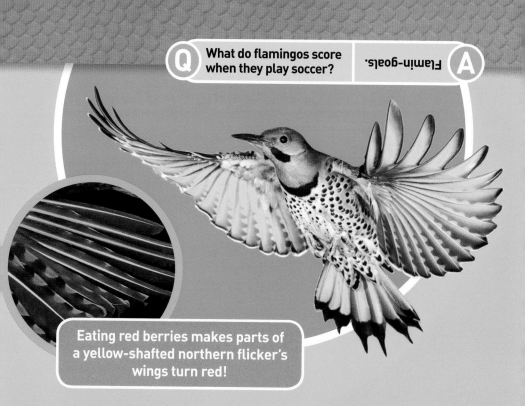

Q What do flamingos score when they play soccer?

A Flamin-goals.

Eating red berries makes parts of a yellow-shafted northern flicker's wings turn red!

Few animals are as famous for their color as the pink flamingo. But pink isn't this bird's true color.

Flamingo chicks have gray or white feathers. It takes two years for their feathers to change. The algae (AL-jee) and shrimp they eat turn their feathers pink.

aeolid nudibranch

Another kind of animal famous for its borrowed colors is the nudibranch (NOO-duh-brank). Its body absorbs and then shows the colors of the animals it eats. This lets it hide among its prey while it feeds.

Cool Color Word

PREY: An animal that is eaten by other animals

As this dorid nudibranch eats a red sponge, it absorbs the red color and turns red itself.

Not all animals can change color. But for those that do, changing color can be the key to survival!

QUIZ WHIZ

How much do you know about animals that change color? After reading this book, probably a lot! Take this quiz and find out.

Answers are at the bottom of page 31.

Which animal's colors change with its moods?

A. puffin
B. snowshoe hare
C. chameleon
D. Dalmatian

1

In which season do some Arctic animals have white coats?

2

A. winter
B. spring
C. summer
D. fall

A newborn silvered leaf monkey has _____ fur.

A. black
B. silver
C. brown
D. orange

3

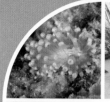

4 Which of these animals has hidden colors?

A. nudibranch
B. arctic fox
C. blue morpho butterfly
D. harp seal

5 What makes a golden tortoise beetle change color?

A. It gets older.
B. It squeezes and relaxes muscles.
C. It responds to a change in the amount of sunlight.
D. It drains the liquid from its shell.

6 A _____ changes color because of what it eats.

A. flamingo
B. squid
C. octopus
D. swan

7 What does camouflage help animals do?

A. stand out
B. blend in
C. see predators
D. attract a mate

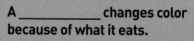

ABSORB: To take in

CAMOUFLAGE: Colors or patterns that help something blend in with its environment

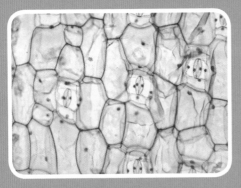

CELLS: The building blocks of living things like plants and animals

PREDATOR: An animal that hunts and eats other animals

PREY: An animal that is eaten by other animals

REFLECT: To bounce back

NATIONAL GEOGRAPHIC
KIDS READERS
for curious kids at every reading level!

DO YOU WANT TO BE A NATIONAL GEOGRAPHIC KIDS SUPER READER?

Go to natgeokids.com/superreaders to download a free poster and learn more about the program. The more you read, the more prizes you earn, including stickers, T-shirt iron-ons, bookmarks, and much more!

National Geographic Kids Readers
for curious kids at every reading level!

Pre-reader • Ready to read

Level 1 Co-reader • Starting to read together

Level 1 • Starting to read

LEVEL 2

Reading independently

Level 2 books are perfect for kids who are ready for longer sentences and more complex vocabulary. New words are defined on the page, but occasional adult help might be welcome.

Level 3 • Fluent reader

BE A NATIONAL GEOGRAPHIC KIDS SUPER READER!

* EARN AWESOME PRIZES
* PLAY BRAIN-BUSTING GAMES
* TAKE CRAZY QUIZZES
* HAVE TOTALLY OUTRAGEOUS FUN!

Watch a fun video and get started at

NATGEOKIDS.COM/SUPERREADERS

EXPLORATION HAPPENS
because of you.

When you read with us, you help further the work of our scientists, explorers, and educators around the world.

Parents, to learn more, visit natgeo.com/info

$4.99 U.S. / $6.99 CAN
ISBN 978-1-4263-3709-3 / PRINTED IN U.S.A.

50499

9 781426 337093